HELPLINE
TEEN ISSUES AND ANSWERS ™

SELF-INJURY AND CUTTING

STOPPING THE PAIN

JOHN M. SHEA, MD

ROSEN
PUBLISHING®

New York

Published in 2014 by The Rosen Publishing Group, Inc.
29 East 21st Street, New York, NY 10010

First Edition

Library of Congress Cataloging-in-Publication Data

Shea, John M.
Self-injury and cutting : stopping the pain/John M. Shea, M.D.—First edition.
     pages cm.—(Helpline : teen issues and answers)
Includes bibliographical references and index.
ISBN 978-1-4488-9448-2 (library binding)
1. Self-mutilation—Juvenile literature. 2. Self-injurious behavior—Juvenile
literature. 3.Teenagers—Mental health—Juvenile literature. 4. College students—
Mental health. I. Title.
RJ506.S44S54 2014
616.85'82—dc23

                                                                    2012047198

Manufactured in the United States of America

CPSIA Compliance Information: Batch #S13YA: For further information, contact Rosen Publishing, New York, New York, at 1-800-237-9932.

CONTENTS

Every day, millions of teenagers and young adults suffer from powerful emotions such as sadness, guilt, and anger. These emotions can become over-whelming and make it next to impossible for them to deal with the pressures of everyday life. Some may feel that the only way they can deal with these feel-ings is to replace the emotional pain with physical pain: they deliberately hurt themselves. They under-stand that purposefully injuring their bodies is not a healthy behavior. Yet for many, the physical pain from self-injury is the only way they know to get relief from tormenting emotions.

Many of those that self-injure suffer silently. Although they are in emotional turmoil, they often succeed in hiding their feelings from the outside world. Because of fear or shame, they may also hide their self-harming behavior. As a result, there is not a lot of reliable information available about who self-injures and why they do so. This has led to some misconceptions about cutting and self-injury. Some people believe that self-injury is merely a "cry for attention." Others think that people who deliberately hurt themselves must be suicidal. Both of these statements could not be further from the truth.

Self-injury may be a hidden problem, but it is also a common one. The Cornell Research Program on Self-Injurious Behavior (CRPSIB), a leader in self-injury research, estimates that up to 17 percent of young adults have deliberately injured themselves at

Behind the physical pain of self-injury there often lies overwhelming emotional pain from anxiety, anger, or depression.

least once by the time they reach college. Self-injury is not only a problem for teenagers. Children as young as age seven or eight and older adults also deliberately hurt themselves.

Self-injury has many serious consequences. People that self-harm are at serious risk of permanently damaging their bodies. Their self-esteem, often already poor, worsens as self-injury feeds into a cycle of shame, guilt, and social isolation. Relying on self-injury to deal with stress and emotional problems does not work in the long term. Using it as a coping strategy can make dealing with other problems later in life more difficult. Adults who continue to self-harm are at a higher risk of committing suicide.

With the high prevalence of self-injury among teenagers and young adults, there is a good chance that you know someone who is deliberately hurting himself or herself. Perhaps you have a friend that you suspect may be self-injuring. Or perhaps you injure yourself deliberately but do not completely understand why. Here, we will explore the hidden world of self-injury, including what may drive some people to harm themselves and how to seek help for yourself or for a friend. It is hoped that with greater understanding and awareness those that self-harm can get the strength and the support they need to stop the cycle of self-injury.

What Is Self-Injury?

CHAPTER 1

There are many different terms that are used to describe the action of deliberately hurting oneself: self-injury, self-harm, and self-inflicted violence. These terms largely refer to the same behavior—deliberately hurting one's body in a way that is serious enough to do damage (such as leaving a scar). This deliberate harm is usually done alone, although some people may harm themselves in a group setting. Some doctors use the term "self-mutilation" because it suggests harming the body without trying to commit suicide, while "self-harm," "self-injury," or "self-inflicted violence" could be used to describe suicide attempts as well as nonsuicidal behaviors. In the following sections, all of these terms refer to nonsuicidal self-injury.

An important part of the definition of self-injury is that there is no intention to commit suicide. In fact,

Tattoos and Body Piercings

Are tattoos and body piercings a form of self-injury? After all, both do damage to the body. Tattooing uses tiny needles to deposit ink into the skin and is often quite painful. Piercings can be very painful as well: holes are created in the body, and objects are placed in those holes to prevent them from healing as they normally would.

Despite this, tattooing and piercing are not considered self-injury because of the reasons why people engage in these behaviors. Those who receive tattoos or piercings do it for aesthetic reasons. They believe the procedures will make their bodies more distinctive and attractive. The pain is usually an undesired consequence. In contrast, for those that self-injure, the pain is the main reason for the behavior. The physical pain helps them feel better emotionally.

With this difference in mind, it is important to note that there may be overlaps between the groups. Tattoos and piercings are considered allowable and even desirable in most cultures, while self-injury is frowned upon and shameful. Therefore, some people may use tattooing and piercings as a substitute for cutting or other forms of self-harm.

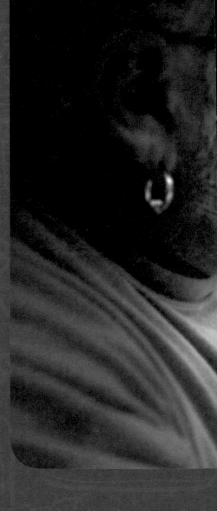

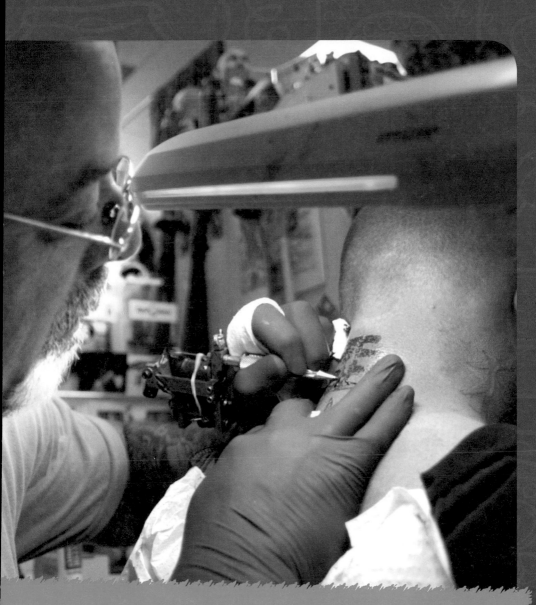

For some people, tattoos and piercings are ways to express themselves. In most cases, these body modifications are not considered self-injury.

many of those who self-injure say that hurting themselves often relieves the tensions and pressures they feel to kill themselves. That is to say, they self-injure in order to escape suicidal thoughts. Sadly, self-injury is a short-term fix for long-term problems, and many young people who have harmed themselves eventually attempt suicide. According to an article in the *American Journal of Psychiatry,* those that self-injure are up to thirty-four times more likely to kill themselves than those in the general population.

METHODS OF SELF-INJURY

The most common method of self-injury is cutting. Cutting is using a sharp object, such as a knife, razor blade, or a piece of glass, to deliberately scratch or cut skin. Cutting is sometimes referred to as slicing or slashing. Since it is the most common method, the term "cutting" is sometimes used synonymously with "self-injury."

Banging or punching is the second most common self-harming behavior. This involves hitting oneself with fists or a hard object, such as a hammer. Sometimes, bangers throw their bodies against a floor or a wall. One extreme form of banging includes bone breaking, in which a person uses a hard object to break one of his or her bones. Cutting tends to be more common in young women, while males are more likely to hit themselves.

Cutting is the most common form of self-injury among women. To keep the scars—and the behavior—hidden, people typically injure areas of the body normally covered with clothing.

Another method of self-injury involves burning oneself with something hot, such as a lit cigarette, matches, or a curling iron. Some people bite themselves on the arms, fingers, or lips. Others suffer from trichotillomania, or a strong desire to pull out their own hair. Hair is pulled not only from the scalp, but also from eyebrows or eyelashes.

Some people purposefully aggravate their wounds to prevent them from healing. This may include removing stitches early, sticking foreign objects in a wound, or picking at a wound that is healing. While some people, especially younger children, pick at scabs, this is not necessarily an act of self-injury. Self-injury is the deliberate intention to do yourself harm. Picking at a scab because of boredom or because it is itchy is not self-injury. Picking at a scab because you do not want it to heal is self-injury.

These methods of self-injury are not mutually exclusive. That is, a person may perform more than one of these methods. According to an article in *Pediatrics*, about 70 percent of college-age students who repeatedly self-injure use more than one method.

The same article reports that the arms are the most common locations injured, followed by hands, wrists, thighs, and stomach. Because self-harmers try to keep their behaviors and injuries a secret, these locations make sense, as they are easily hidden. About one in ten self-harmers deliberately injure their head or their fingers.

Who Performs Self-Injury?

CHAPTER 2

It is difficult to get accurate information about who performs self-injury.
A common trait among people
who self-harm is that they often
try to hide their injuries and their
behaviors. Indeed, many cases are
discovered only when the injuries
become serious enough to need a
doctor's attention. Among health care
providers, there is no requirement to report cases of self-
injury to a national agency, as there is for some
diseases.

PREVALENCE OF SELF-INJURY

Much of our knowledge about self-injury comes from sur-
veys and interviews. However, this approach relies on the
honesty and openness of the people surveyed. In addition, it examines only a small portion of a much larger
population. Therefore, it is important to remember that

The adolescent years can be stressful for many as they face powerful social and academic pressures. Because the behavior usually occurs in private, identifying who is turning to self-injury can be difficult.

most statistics about self-injury are only estimates and may in fact underestimate the number of people who self-injure.

Researchers at CRPSIB conducted a survey of American college students in 2006. The study found that about 17 percent of students had performed at least one act of self-injury, and about 11 percent had engaged in repeated self-injury (two or more times). Similar numbers have been found in Canada and Europe. The Child and Adolescent Self-Harm in Europe (CASE) Study, published in 2008, found that three out of ten young women and one out of ten young men had deliberately harmed or had planned to harm themselves within the previous year. The American Self-Harm Information Clearinghouse (ASHIC) estimates that between two and three million Americans over the age of twelve intentionally harm themselves each year.

While some experts believe that women are more likely to self-injure than men, self-injury is not uncommon among males. Indeed, the CRPSIB suggests that the number of men who self-injure might be the same as women, but that men are less likely to admit the behavior or be discovered.

#

In most instances, self-harming behavior starts during adolescence, between the ages of twelve and fifteen. For some people, this is a period of great emotional stress. Adolescents often start to question their own identity— who they are individually and in relation to family and friends. Friends and peers become especially important, and fitting in and finding acceptance can cause great anxiety.

Princess Diana

Diana, Princess of Wales, was a beloved member of the British royal family. After her marriage to Prince Charles in 1981, she won respect and admiration worldwide not only for her beauty and style, but also for her many charitable activities. She used her resources to help those less fortunate, including the homeless and people living with HIV/AIDS.

During an interview on the BBC television program *Panorama* in November 1995, Princess Diana admitted that she had a difficult time dealing with her role in the royal family and in the public eye. After the birth of her first son, William, Diana suffered from postpartum depression. Around this time, she started to injure herself.

"When no one listens to you, or you feel no one's listening to you, all sorts of things start to happen," Diana told interviewer Martin Bashir. "For instance you have so much pain inside yourself that you try and hurt yourself on the outside because you want help, but it's the wrong help you're asking for. I didn't like myself; I was ashamed because I couldn't cope with the pressures."

In audio tape recordings she made for biographer Andrew Morton, Diana confessed that at times, she hated herself because she didn't think herself worthy. She said, "I was trying to cut my wrists with razor blades...we were trying to hide that from everybody...I was just so desperate." Other times, she said, she threw herself down stairs and cut herself in her chest and thighs with a penknife.

With her honesty and courage in speaking publicly about her struggles with self-injury, Diana reminded the world that anyone, even a beloved and beautiful princess, can suffer from low self-esteem and crippling emotional pain.

In the eyes of many people at the time, Princess Diana seemed to live a perfect fairytale life. In reality, she suffered from the same feelings of self-doubt and self-hatred that plague so many worldwide.

Adolescence is also a time when romantic and sexual feelings and relationships become more important. This can be a confusing period for many teenagers, especially when they receive mixed messages from media advertisements, celebrities, families, and peers. At the same time, adolescents often seek to become more independent. As a consequence, they may find it difficult to talk about the stresses and confusion in their lives with

Teens often struggle to find acceptance by their peers and become more independent from their parents. Sometimes, however, this can cause them to feel isolated when dealing with emotional problems.

parents or other family members. Unfortunately, they may turn to self-injury as a way to calm themselves and cope with stress.

The stresses that young children experience can be just as difficult as the stresses adolescents face. Peer pressure, gossiping, and especially bullying can all result in emotional pain. As a result, some children begin to hurt themselves deliberately as early as age seven. A study conducted by the University of Denver found that 7.6 percent of third graders had deliberately harmed themselves at least once.

Most—but not all—people who self-harm stop as they enter adulthood. According to CRPSIB, self-injury is a cyclical behavior. In other words, people who deliberately self-harm may stop for a while but suddenly start doing it again years later, especially during times of increased stress. According to an article in the *International Journal of Geriatric Psychiatry*, older adults who continue to self-harm are at a much higher risk for suicide than young adults who self-harm.

COMMON TRAITS

There appear to be some traits in common among those who deliberately self-harm. Examining these traits may help us understand why some people feel the need to hurt themselves. It is important to remember that while these traits may be common among self-injurers, they are not found in 100 percent of those who self-injure.

Poor self-image, including shame and self-hatred, is a common trait among those that deliberately harm themselves.

Many people who deliberately harm their bodies have poor self-esteem and actively dislike themselves. The CASE Study found that the lower a person's self-esteem, the more severe his or her history of self-injury was. Anger directed inward and shame are also common among self-harmers (although people can be good at hiding these emotions). Clinical depression is another characteristic that appears frequently in those who self-injure. Similar to the data on low self-esteem, the CASE Study found that the more depressed someone was, the more often he or she engaged in self-injury.

People who self-injure tend to be—but are not always—aggressive and impulsive. They do not plan well for the future. This may be because they do not think of themselves as powerful or believe that they exercise much control over their lives. They can also be irritable, often getting upset when minor things go wrong. Many times, self-injurers do not have effective skills for dealing with stress.

It is important to keep in mind that people who deliberately self-injure are not "crazy" or insane. In most cases their thoughts are just as sane as those of people who have no desire to hurt themselves. Self-injurers act and appear like everyone else. Their friends and families often have no idea of the emotional pain that their loved one suffers.

Self-injury is a behavior that some people use to deal with the emotional pain they feel inside.

to be independent and to be accepted by their peers can make them reluctant to discuss difficult problems with parents or friends.

As a result, the depression, anger, guilt, or anxiety can build up. Many teens who self-injure experience such powerful and overwhelming emotions that they find it difficult to continue their lives normally. They find that harming themselves provides temporary relief. The pain from the injury provides a distraction from their dark thoughts and offers a brief release from their emotions. People who self-injure often tell therapists and researchers that after the initial pain, they feel more peaceful and calm.

Everyone has experienced guilt, sadness, stress, and other powerful emotions, and most try to handle them with the coping skills they have learned in life. Some coping mechanisms, such as going for a long run or talking to a friend or therapist, can be helpful and healthful. Others, such as alcohol abuse, drug abuse, or self-injury, are unhealthy and unhelpful. These methods only help people temporarily ignore the problems; they don't make them go away. At the same time, these unhealthy coping mechanisms harm the body, sometimes permanently, and ultimately create new and potentially deadly problems.

PUNISHMENT

Some people intentionally hurt themselves because the injuries and pain serve as forms of punishment. Some people suffer from overwhelming guilt, shame, or anger at themselves. These feelings can turn into self-hatred that is so powerful that it can be unbearable to live with. Punishing themselves with self-inflicted pain provides temporary relief from these feelings.

Many self-injurers suffer from poor self-esteem. People who have very low self-esteem are more likely to

Sadly, some people wrongly believe that they deserve the pain from self-inflicted cuts and burns because they are unworthy and must be punished.

feel overwhelming shame and self-hatred. Many self-injurers suffer from poor self-esteem. Sometimes, this is because they grow up in an environment in which their thoughts, opinions, and feelings are not important. Researchers refer to this as an "invalidating environment." In this situation, when a child expresses himself or herself, a parent, guardian, or another authority figure dismisses or ignores the child's ideas and often belittles him or her in the process. Phrases common in an invalidating environment include:

- "You always ask such stupid questions."
- "Stop being so sensitive all the time."
- "You're such a liar."
- "Don't you ever stop talking?"
- "You are overreacting, as always."
- "Stop crying! Get over it."

While we all have heard phrases like this occasionally, hearing them constantly can cause a child to believe that nothing he or she thinks or feels is important. The child may begin to believe that he or she is not worthy of attention or love. The resulting shame and self-hatred can prompt some people to injure themselves as a form of self-punishment. Other people that have experienced an invalidating or abusive environment might experiment with self-harm as a form of self-expression. When someone is taught that expressing his or her feelings is "bad," self-injury can provide a way to release bottled-up emotions.

Self-Injury and Childhood Abuse

Unfortunately, many people who injure their bodies as teenagers and young adults were abused as children. Abuse can take many forms, including sexual abuse, physical abuse, or neglect. Neglect occurs when parents or guardians do not satisfy the basic needs of a child under their care. This neglect can be physical (not providing adequate food or shelter) or emotional (not providing a warm and supportive environment). Examples of emotional neglect can include constantly belittling a child, isolating a child by severely limiting his or her social contact outside the house, and refusing to show the child affection. According to an article in the *Canadian Journal of Psychiatry*, children who are emotionally neglected are more likely to self-harm later in life.

Physical or sexual abuse is also common among people who self-injure. The *Journal of Traumatic Stress* reports that more than half of college students who self-injure were sexually abused as children. Physical and sexual abuse can create traumatic memories and overwhelming emotions that the victims may find difficult to deal with, even years after the abuse has ended. Sadly, sexual abuse is often committed by a person that a child knows, and the abuse violates the victim's trust. This betrayal of trust can harm the victim's ability to handle and cope with difficult emotions and situations. The trauma of abuse can lead victims into a permanent state of fearfulness and anxiety. Self-injury often gives child abuse victims a small sense of control over their own lives and temporarily releases that fear and anxiety.

TO FEEL ALIVE

Some people say they deliberately hurt themselves to try to make themselves feel "more alive." People who self-injure for this reason often say they feel detached or distant from the world. They describe themselves as feeling empty inside. In contrast to the situations described above, these people may not feel much emotion at all.

While this may sound quite different from self-harming for feeling too much emotion, there is much in common among these groups. Some people live through horrible experiences, such as getting hurt in a car accident, watching a close family member die, or living though physical or sexual abuse. The memories from these experiences can be so terrifying and painful that they become unbearable. In some cases, these traumas can cause people to block out these memories and feelings as a coping mechanism. Their bad memories may be hidden to stop the pain, but some of their other emotions, even the good ones such as joy and excitement, may be dulled, too. This may create the detached and empty feeling that some people experience.

When such people hurt themselves, they often describe the experience as like a shock or like waking up. The pain from self-injury makes them feel more alive and whole once again. Like people who hurt themselves because of too much sadness, anger, or guilt, they also have difficulty dealing with their emotions, so they turn to the pain of self-injury to help them cope.

The desire to fit into a group is strong for everyone, not just adolescents. Unfortunately, this desire can lead some to do things they shouldn't, including harming themselves.

PEER PRESSURE

Among the main reasons why people deliberately self-harm, certain characteristics seem to be common— namely, emotional distress in their lives and no satisfactory way of coping with that distress. There are some groups of self-harmers that do not fit this profile, however.

Some teens harm themselves, not to find emotional relief, but rather to fit in socially. Some people might start the behavior because their boyfriend or girlfriend is doing it. Others might start because they want to appear hip, bold, or goth. Still others might do it because they feel pressure from their peers. These people might cut and harm themselves to fit into a group or to avoid being bullied or ridiculed. When a person cuts because someone else is doing it, it is referred to as copycat cutting. Psychologists also refer to this phenomenon as social contagion.

Self-Injury and Mental Health

CHAPTER 4

For many years, mental health experts had not considered self-injury a disease. Rather, the American Psychiatry Association (APA) had considered it merely a symptom of other problems, such as depression or personality disorders. Indeed, there was a widespread belief that most people who cut themselves had a personality disorder. As research into the hidden world of self-injury uncovers more information, it is now understood that only a small percentage of cutters suffer from a personality disorder. The *Diagnostic and Statistical Manual of Mental Disorders (DSM)* is the manual all physicians and mental health workers use to diagnose mental problems. With the publication of the fifth edition of the manual in 2013, nonsuicidal self-injury was classified as a mental health disorder for the first time.

Although self-injury is now considered a disorder in itself, it still remains a symptom of some other disorders as well. These disorders are often associated with intense emotions and compulsions that can lead some people to harm themselves for temporary relief.

PERSONALITY DISORDERS

Some people who engage in self-injury have a personality disorder. People with personality disorders think and deal with situations in a way that is very strict and unhealthy. They tend to have a narrow way of dealing with the world and do not adapt well to new situations. Because their thoughts and behaviors are so inflexible, they often come into conflict with other people. Those with personality disorders often think that their thoughts and behaviors are "right" and "normal" and may blame others for their problems. The traits associated with personality disorders usually appear around adolescence and continue throughout adulthood, although they tend to become less pronounced during middle age. According to the National Institutes of Mental Health (NIMH), about 9 percent of the U.S. population has a personality disorder, such as borderline personality disorder (BPD).

With borderline personality disorder, a person tends to view the world in extremes: someone or something is either very good or very bad. The person's views may change rapidly and with little cause. A person with BPD may enjoy someone's company one minute and then become angry and resentful of that person a few hours later.

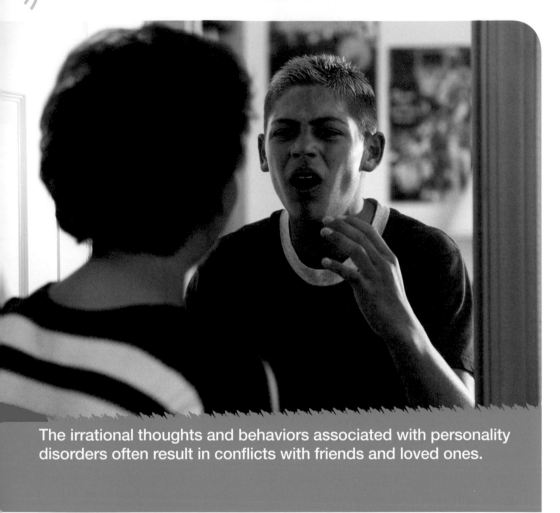

The irrational thoughts and behaviors associated with personality disorders often result in conflicts with friends and loved ones.

Those with BPD are often uncertain about their own identity and try to define themselves through other people. They can become very dependent, obsessive, and clingy in a romantic relationship. There is often anxiety and fear that a loved one will abandon him or her. According to NIMN, about 1.4 percent of the American population has BPD.

In keeping with their rapidly changing views, people with BPD can be very impulsive, especially with regard to sexual encounters and drug use. They tend to be very dramatic, making situations more intense than they need to be and starting crises on purpose. Sometimes, those with BPD will react in irrational ways, such as yelling for no reason or starting fires, which can push their loved ones away.

Mental health experts have agreed that there are a number of traits that are common among those with BPD. In order to be diagnosed with BPD, someone must have five of the following nine traits:

- Fear of abandonment
- A pattern of unstable relationships
- Poor self-esteem
- Impulsiveness
- Intense mood swings
- Feeling "empty" inside
- Intense flashes of anger
- Periods of feeling removed from reality
- A history of self-injury

Because adolescence is a time when many teenagers experiment with new identities and behaviors, mental health experts do not officially diagnose someone with BPD or other personality disorders until he or she is over eighteen years of age. However, the unhealthy traits of the disorder are usually present by age fifteen.

DEPRESSION

Another common mental health problem associated with self-injury is depression. Depression is not merely feeling sad. Everyone feels down sometimes. That is a normal feeling, and most people will feel better after a short time. Some people get very sad, however, to the point that they feel life is hopeless. Few things can cheer them up, and if something does, the sadness soon returns. Some people may not feel sad during a depressive episode. Instead, they may feel frustration or anger. These dark emotions can last for weeks or months. The feelings become so strong and powerful that they overwhelm the person suffering from depression, making it impossible to lead a normal life.

Mental health experts look for these common characteristics when diagnosing depression:

- Feeling sad, frustrated, or angry every day
- No longer enjoying things that used to be fun, such as a hobby
- Changes in weight or appetite (eating much more or less than usual)
- Changes in sleep (sleeping much more or less than usual)
- Feeling tired or restless all the time
- Feeling hopeless, worthless, or guilty all the time
- Difficulty concentrating and making decisions
- Thoughts of death and suicide

Depression involves overwhelming feelings of sadness, anger, frustration, or hopelessness that interfere with a person's ability to live a normal life.

While self-injury is not an official symptom that defines depression, the CASE Study has shown that many people who self-injure are depressed. As we have seen, many people who deliberately hurt themselves do so to escape overwhelming feelings, especially sadness, guilt, or anger. These feelings are common among those with depression. Some people with depression use self-injury as a coping mechanism to distract

Self-Injury and Eating Disorders

Eating disorders are illnesses that affect one's everyday diet. One type of eating disorder, anorexia nervosa, is characterized by the urge to eat extremely small amounts of food in order to stay thin. Most of the time, people with anorexia nervosa are already very thin, but they have an unrealistic view of their own bodies and try to keep their weight at dangerously low levels.

Bulimia nervosa is an eating disorder in which people may eat an excessive amount of food. They may feel out of control or guilty about this binge eating and then try to compensate for the large meal or snacking episode. Compensation may include vomiting to empty the stomach of food, taking medications to help lose weight, or excessively exercising to burn extra calories. In contrast to those with anorexia nervosa, people with bulimia nervosa are often at a normal weight or slightly overweight. Similar to anorexia, those with bulimia are obsessed about their weight.

Eating disorders generally begin during adolescence. According to NIMH, about 2.7 percent of teenagers between ages thirteen and eighteen will develop a serious eating disorder. Young women are two and a half times more likely to have an eating disorder than young men.

In a study at Stanford University, over 40 percent of people with an eating disorder admitted to self-harming behaviors. Scientists believe that people with eating disorders have a high level of anxiety because of their obsession with food. Cutting and other self-harming behaviors may offer a relief from that anxiety. In addition, those with eating disorders often suffer from self-hatred because of their poor body image and self-esteem, and they may use self-injury as a way to punish themselves.

themselves from these emotions, exchanging physical pain for their emotional suffering.

POST-TRAUMATIC STRESS DISORDER

In post-traumatic stress disorder (PTSD), someone who lives through a frightening or stressful event becomes very anxious afterward, even when he or she is perfectly safe. The frightening event, such as being involved in an automobile accident, surviving a natural disaster, or being a kidnapping victim, may have been life threatening. Military personnel returning from combat can develop PTSD. Victims of physical or sexual abuse often develop PTSD as well.

People affected by PTSD suffer from intrusive and distressing thoughts and memories. These memories are inescapable and can make sufferers feel as if they are reliving their horrible experiences. As a result, they feel anxious, irritable, and angry. Those with PTSD often have trouble sleeping. Their anxiety makes it difficult for them to relax, and they often have nightmares.

Some people with PTSD develop what mental health experts call avoidance. Because the emotions surrounding the traumatic event can be overwhelming, some people "dial down" their emotions and do not allow themselves to feel anything. This emotional numbing has a negative effect on the lives of those with PTSD. People with the avoidance symptoms of PTSD have great difficulty expressing themselves to their loved ones. They find

Military personnel returning from combat may suffer from PTSD, making it difficult for them to resume their civilian lives.

they cannot be loving or tender, and they may begin to isolate themselves from others. Similar to the symptoms found in depression, they have difficulty expressing happiness and joy, and they avoid hobbies and other activities that once made them happy.

Another common trait of those with PTSD is survivor's guilt. Survivor's guilt may occur after a person lives through a terrible experience in which other people died. Some military personnel experience survivor's guilt after they witness other soldiers or innocent civilians die during combat. Indeed, according to an article in *USA TODAY*, 7 percent of Marines returning from combat in Afghanistan have symptoms of PTSD, and many of their symptoms seem linked to survivor's guilt.

According to a review in *Psychiatric Services*, patients suffering from PTSD are more likely than the general population to engage in self-harming behavior. Since these patients typically suffer from overwhelming guilt, anxiety, sadness, and emotional numbness, it becomes understandable why some might turn to self-injury as a coping mechanism to deal with their emotional distress.

The Dangers of Self-Injury

CHAPTER 5

Psychiatrists and other mental health experts separate self-injury from a more deadly form of self-harm—suicide attempts. In a suicide attempt, a person decides to harm himself or herself so seriously that he or she could die. In self-injury, the intention is not to kill oneself but rather to deal with emotional distress. The goal may be to cause enough pain to distract from overwhelming feelings of sadness or frustration. Or, the pain may be meant to "shock" someone who is feeling numb into feeling alive again. Regardless of the specific reasons, self-harming behaviors are often performed so someone can continue living life.

PHYSICAL CONSEQUENCES

Even if the intention is not to permanently harm oneself, there are serious, and sometimes deadly, risks to self-injuring behaviors.

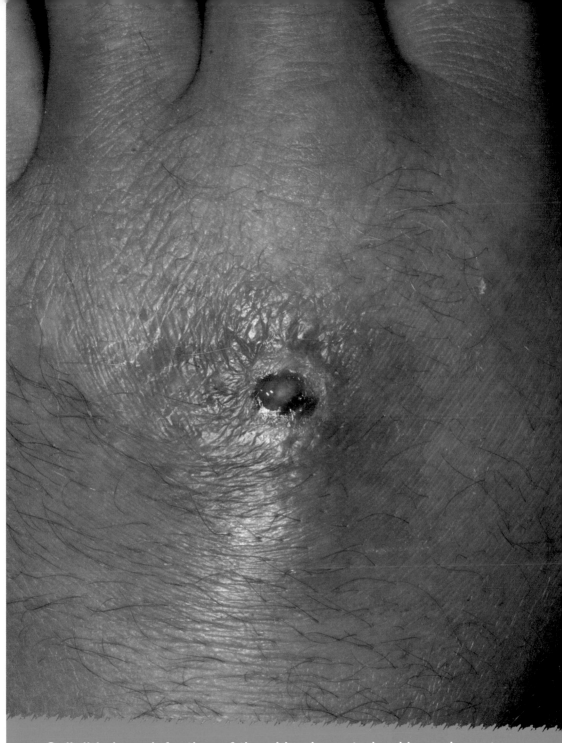

Cellulitis is an infection of the skin characterized by redness, warmth, pain, and swelling. Damage to the skin from cuts, burns, and other self-injuries can cause severe cellulitis.

A common consequence of cutting is infection. The skin is an important barrier against germs such as bacteria and viruses. Cutting the skin breaks down that barrier and allows germs to enter deeper into the body. This is especially true if the object being used for cutting is not sterilized. The infection may be limited to the skin around the cuts (this type of skin infection is known as cellulitis). But germs that invade past the skin can cause the whole body to become diseased, resulting in fever, shock, and even death. Because of these risks, some infections may require treatment with antibiotics and hospitalization.

Another complication from cutting may occur when a person cuts too deep. Important body parts beneath the skin can be injured, which can lead to permanent injury or death. For example, the forearm is a common location used for cutting. An important blood vessel known as the radial artery runs in the forearm just beneath the skin. (This is the artery that is used to check a pulse at the wrist.) The blood in the arteries is under high pressure, and if an artery is cut, a lot of blood can be lost very quickly. Repairing an artery may require surgery. A badly damaged artery that is not repaired could cause someone to go into shock, and the heart and brain might not get enough oxygen.

In addition to harming blood vessels, cutting or other acts of self-injury can damage nerves, muscles, tendons, and ligaments. Muscles, ligaments, and tendons provide structure and allow body parts to move. For example, the muscles and tendons in the forearm allow the wrist to move back and forth. If these were cut, control of the wrist would be lost until surgery could repair the damage. If nerves were damaged, the effects could be permanent. This could mean the loss of the sense of touch on one arm or hand.

Banging and pounding is another common form of self-injury, especially among young men. While not much research has been dedicated to brain injury during self-harm, it is now well understood that even minor hits to the head, such as collisions during sports, can have serious effects on the brain. Repeated brain injuries can affect memory, language, and emotions. According to the Centers for Disease Control and Prevention (CDC), repeated head injuries increase the risk for neurological diseases such as Alzheimer's disease or Parkinson's disease. Hits to the head can cause damage to the brain that may take years to show up. Repeated brain injuries within a short time period can result in a coma or death.

EMOTIONAL CONSEQUENCES

Besides the physical damage self-injury can cause, there are also emotional consequences. Self-injury is the result of a deeper emotional problem. People use it to escape from emotional numbness, self-hatred and guilt, or overwhelming feelings of sadness, anger, or frustration. While cutting may provide a temporary relief, it does not eliminate the underlying problem. Self-injury is only a

Scars

The most common side effect of self-injury is scarring. Banging, burning, and cutting can all result in scars. While the pain of self-injury is temporary, scars are permanent. Most people who self-harm hide their behavior, and they often feel the need to hide their scars as well. This can lead them to avoid social situations where their skin might be exposed, such as gym class or a day at the beach or pool. This social isolation can lower self-esteem and lead to depression. In turn, this can increase the person's urge to self-harm again.

Some people, including cutters and other self-harmers, believe that scars are not permanent. They believe that cosmetic (or "plastic") surgery can erase scars and repair all the damage done to the skin. This is not correct. While it is true that surgery can minimize some scarring by cutting it out, the procedure only replaces a larger scar with a smaller one. The damage to the skin will never completely disappear. Scarring left from burns is especially difficult to repair.

In addition, cosmetic surgeries can be very costly. Repairing even a small scar can cost hundreds of dollars; repairing many of them can become very expensive. In most instances, the expenses of the surgeries will have to be paid by the patient, as most medical insurance companies will not pay for an elective cosmetic procedure.

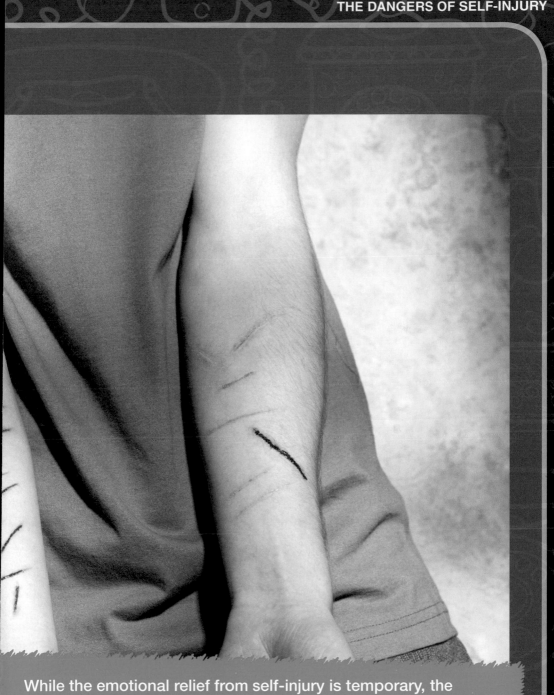

While the emotional relief from self-injury is temporary, the resulting scars are permanent. These scars can become a source of guilt, anxiety, and shame for many self-harmers.

distraction, and the real problems return when the pain subsides.

If the root problems are not addressed directly, they may get worse. Self-injury is not a healthy coping skill, nor is it very effective. When additional problems and stresses arise, as they often do, self-injury will likely not be enough to make someone feel better. He or she might not know how to deal with these new problems. In desperation, he or she may try more dangerous and self-destructive coping mechanisms and escapes, such as alcohol, drugs, or suicide.

Stopping
Self-Injury

CHAPTER 6

Self-injury may provide some relief to powerful emotional distress. Therefore, it becomes difficult to stop this behavior. There is no miracle cure that will instantaneously make someone feel better. There is no quick fix that will take away someone's urges to self-harm. While there are ways to reduce and eliminate this behavior, there is no one cure that will work equally well on everyone. Just as there are different reasons why people self-injure, there are different ways to help them stop the cycle of pain and emotional distress.

Some people stop self-injuring on their own, while others rely on the help of a mental health professional. According to the CRPSIB, the majority (but not all) of the people who self-injure stop within five years of starting. In many cases, these people learn new, more effective coping strategies that allow them to deal with emotional crises. However, self-harming behavior is often cyclical, and some people may start cutting again after many years of abstaining if they encounter a particularly stressful situation.

TAKING THE FIRST STEPS

The first step in ending self-injury is admitting that it is an unhealthy behavior that should be stopped. This is not an easy step. Admitting that one has a serious problem can be difficult, especially when the behavior may momentarily help. It takes wisdom and maturity for someone to look at his or her own life and identify problems. It takes great strength and courage to face the problems and try to fix them.

Admitting the behavior to someone else can be just as difficult. Many self-harmers suffer from poor self-esteem. They might worry what others will think of them if they admit they have a psychological problem. Some, especially victims of past abuse and neglect, might find it difficult to trust someone enough to share this secret. But telling a friend, family member, or therapist has a tremendous advantage: this person becomes an ally in the fight against the self-harming behavior. When life becomes overwhelming and the urge to self-harm seems uncontrollable, it is important to have someone to turn to for support. In addition, this ally can help set up and enforce motivations and consequences for one's actions. For example, the partner can take away a privilege if one self-injures or give a reward if he or she avoids self-harm.

Discussing self-injury with a trusted friend or relative can be an important step toward dealing with the problem.

To make it easier to talk to family members or others about self-injury, consider rehearsing your statements a few times in the mirror. Some people write down their words in the form of a letter. For the discussion, choose a private place where others will not overhear and the conversation will not be rushed. The goal is to be as comfortable as possible. There is no reason to get into graphic details about self-harming, but the conversation should be honest and open. When revealing the problem to others, a confidant, such as a therapist or close friend, can be present to give moral support.

THERAPY

Perhaps the most effective step in ending self-harming behavior is to seek the help of a mental health profes-sional. A therapist can help someone not only stop the pattern of self-injury, but also explore the reasons that drive him or her to do it.

Often, therapy focuses on getting a patient to recog-nize his or her triggering emotions and teaching the person healthier ways to cope. One goal is to break the cycle of repeatedly using self-harm as a response to neg-ative emotions. Another goal is to help the patient understand that the short-term relief self-injury provides is not as effective as facing and dealing with problems in a mature and healthy manner.

Ideally, a therapist will help the patient address the problems that lead to self-injury urges. In some cases, this may involve dealing with communication issues, especially with parents. In other cases, it may involve working to increase self-esteem and treat depression. In still other cases, the therapist may help the person deal with the emotional trauma of physical or sexual abuse.

A therapist should never make anyone feel bad or ashamed because of self-harming behavior. A person should have a high level of trust in his or her therapist and should feel comfortable talking with the therapist about

A therapist, especially one with experience dealing with self-injury, can be a tremendous help in ending self-harming behaviors and learning healthy coping strategies.

his or her thoughts, emotions, and actions. In most cases, what is shared in a therapy session is strictly confidential, with three exceptions: (1) the patient is at risk for seriously hurting himself or herself; (2) the patient is at risk for hurting someone else; or (3) the patient is being harmed by someone else. Outside of these three safety reasons, discussions with a therapist will remain private. The organizations and Web sites listed later provide resources for contacting professionals who specialize in therapy for self-injury.

LEARNING ALTERNATIVE COPING MECHANISMS

Because stopping the powerfully ingrained behavior of self-injury right away is not always possible, some therapists start by getting their patients to delay the self-harming behavior for a period of time (for example, sixty seconds). Gradually, the therapist and the patient work to increase that time delay. Eventually, the impulse to self-harm decreases, and newer coping mechanisms begin to work.

In the beginning, there can be a lot of frustration, as new coping mechanisms may not seem to provide as much relief as self-injury did. But it is important to stay committed and keep practicing the new, healthier behaviors. These behaviors may include calling a friend or a therapist, taking slow and deep breaths, taking a long walk, screaming into a pillow, doing yoga poses, or petting an animal.

If the urge to hurt oneself becomes unbearable, there are other ways to make the body uncomfortable without damaging it. For example, try holding an ice cube until it melts or eating a lemon. Replacing self-injury with these behaviors is not a long-term fix, but it may relieve the urge to self-harm without the scars and damage. In addition, these actions do not cause the shame or guilt that self-injury does.

Journaling is a great way to organize thoughts and examine problems that may be causing stress. Sometimes problems don't seem as unmanageable after they are written down.

Some people who are trying to end their self-harming behaviors find it useful to keep a journal. Journals allow their authors to explore what is going on in their lives, the emotions they are feeling, and their reactions to them. Journals may be useful for identifying certain patterns, especially pinpointing the kinds of situations that give them the urge to self-harm.

Another method a therapist may try is known as extinction therapy. In this form of therapy, the therapist and patient talk about the self-harming behavior constantly for several sessions in a row. Eventually, the patient may become tired of talking about the behavior and then become tired of the behavior itself.

Hospital-based treatments are usually used as a last resort. For example, someone who is self-injuring might be admitted to a hospital if he or she is doing serious damage to the body or if there is a concern he or she might be suicidal. Hospitals may provide some protection and a temporary escape from the patient's problems and stresses. However, for someone to stop self-injuring completely, eventually he or she needs to face and cope with these problems.

HELP FROM OTHERS

To succeed in stopping self-harming behavior, one of the best strategies is to build a strong support network of people. This network should include therapists and other mental health professionals, family members,

Self-Injury and Brain Chemistry

It is clear that events in a person's life (for example, being a victim of sexual abuse or in a terrible car accident) can lead someone to engage in self-injurious behavior. There is evidence that biology also plays a role.

A study conducted by the University of Washington has shown that young women who cut tend to have lower levels of serotonin compared to the general population. Serotonin is a neurotransmitter, and it is often associated with mood. People with depression also have lower levels of serotonin, so perhaps it is not surprising that antidepressant medications are sometimes used to help treat cases of self-injury. However, taking antidepressants, especially selective serotonin reuptake inhibitors (SSRIs), can increase the likelihood that teenagers will engage in self-injurious behavior or even suicide attempts. For this reason, physicians seldom prescribe antidepressant medications to treat self-harming behavior in teens.

In addition, researchers now understand that brain chemicals known as endorphins are released during cutting. Endorphins are natural hormones released by the brain and nervous system in response to pain. They can help take away pain, and in higher amounts they can make someone feel good. This may explain why many cutters report they don't feel much pain during self-harming acts. It may also explain the sense of comfort and well-being that some people feel after harming themselves. Indeed, researchers are now wondering if self-harming behaviors can be addictive. According to the CRPSIB, people that self-harm may become dependent on the endorphin release that occurs during the process. When they stop, they may experience withdrawal symptoms, which may prompt them to engage in more self-harming behaviors.

and friends. These people can be a source of strength when life becomes difficult.

It is important for the self-harming individual and members of the support network to be honest and open with each other. It is a good idea to have a list of at

Having a support network made up of family members, therapists, and good friends can be a source of strength for those dealing with overwhelming emotional problems.

least two people to call if the urge to self-injure begins to appear. These people can provide a distraction from the urges and help the individual deal with the triggers that brought about the urges.

Group therapy and group meetings can also be a tremendous help. Often it is extremely comforting for people to hear others talking about the same problems they are experiencing. Understanding that one is not the only person with powerful urges to self-harm, and seeing others who have conquered those urges, can be a source of great courage for a person trying to overcome self-injury.

10 Great Questions TO ASK A THERAPIST

1 Have you dealt with patients who self-injure?

2 If cutting is bad, why do I feel better afterward?

3 What are the likely consequences if I continue these behaviors?

4 How can I learn to be more open with my feelings?

5 Why do I feel depressed most of the time?

6 Could medication help me fight this behavior?

7 What can I do to prevent having the urge to hurt myself?

8 What are some things I can do when I strongly experience this urge?

9 What happens if I still want to harm myself after therapy has ended?

10 What are some things I can do to feel better about myself?

Helping Friends Who Self-Injure

Dealing with people in your life who self-injure may be difficult. They might try to hide their behavior and, as a result, become less open and honest. They might become angry with others for trying to invade their privacy and interfere with their lives. They might even try to convince others that cutting is "cool" and pressure them to do it, too.

DISCUSS THE PROBLEM

The first step in helping a friend or relative who self-injures is recognizing that he or she is engaging in this harmful behavior. This is not necessarily easy, since many people's natural instinct is to pretend there is no problem. It can be very difficult to admit that a friend or loved one is deliberately hurting himself or herself. Many people will try to deny the warning signs they may see, such as scars on a

Talking to a friend about his or her self-harming behavior can be extremely difficult, but it opens up lines of communication that can eventually lead to recovery and healing.

friend's body and unconvincing stories about how she got them. Bringing up the subject of self-injury is very challenging because there is uncertainty about how the person will react. Instead, many people find it easier to avoid talking about it, and some might avoid spending time with a friend because of it.

Realizing that a friend is self-harming can bring up some difficult emotions. It is natural to become a little angry with a friend when you realize he or she has been lying to you about the causes of scars. Some people might feel guilty when they find out a close friend has been self-harming. They might question whether any of their actions contributed to their friend's behavior or whether they could have done something to stop it.

These feelings of denial, anger, and guilt can make it difficult to talk to the friend about his or her problem. But communication is one of the best ways to help him or her. Ignoring the problem feeds into the cycle of hiding it. Open and honest talking can lessen the social isolation many self-harmers feel.

Be available to talk to a friend or family member that self-injures, but never force the topic if he or she does not want to discuss it. Self-harmers are often trying to sort out their own feelings about the behavior. It may take time for the person to feel comfortable discussing it with anyone, even a close friend. Even if you are not talking about self-harm directly, your company may distract your friend from his or her urges.

BE SUPPORTIVE

While discussing self-injury with a friend, try to be supportive and understanding, and avoid making any judgments. Be careful not to belittle any of his or her emotions. Don't say things like, "You shouldn't let such small problems upset you like that." Provide an environment in which your friend can feel safe and free to be open and honest.

Warning Signs of Self-Injury

How can one tell if a friend or family member is self-injuring? Often, it may be difficult. In general, those that self-injure do so in secret. Sometimes, however, there may be clues that a friend is harming himself or herself.

Multiple cuts or burns on the body, usually of different ages, are one sign. People that cut tend to make small incisions that are parallel to each other. Occasionally, they may carve words or symbols in their skin, such as "FAT" or "L" for "loser." If a friend repeatedly has "accidents," that is certainly a cause for concern. Always wearing long-sleeved shirts and a long skirt or pants, even when it may not be appropriate (for example, at a beach or on a hot day), is suspicious as well.

Someone who is self-harming may begin to act differently. Generally, people that self-injure become more socially withdrawn; they may not spend as much time with their friends as they used to. They may seem to lose interest in things and activities that they once enjoyed. They may appear angrier or more irritable.

It may be easier to ignore these warning signs and avoid the challenging conversations that may result from them. But an important part of becoming a responsible adult, and being a good friend, is to make these difficult choices and make your friend's well-being and safety the priority.

Multiple parallel scars of different ages are strong warning signs that someone is deliberately self-harming.

Make sure your friend understands that you can separate him or her from the self-harming behavior. You may love your friend and dislike the behavior at the same time. Offer distractions and alternatives to cutting. For example, tell your friend that the next time he or she feels down or feels like self-harming, you'll take him or her to a movie.

The best way to help a friend who self-injures is to provide emotional support and encourage honest and open communication.

You can make it clear that you do not like the self-harming behavior. You may say things such as, "I don't like it when you cut, and I do not want to be in the same room as you while you do it." On the other hand, do not make ultimatums. Don't say things such as, "I won't be your friend if you cut." Only your friend can change his or her behavior. Others may give support, but the responsibility to conquer the problem ultimately lies with that person. Ultimatums create conflict and stress in a friendship. They can also make someone who self-injures feel guilt and self-hatred, which can actually make him or her want to self-injure more.

Do not expect someone who self-injures to stop overnight. Self-injury probably makes the person feel better in some way, and it may take time for him or her to find a better coping mechanism. Or, the person might not self-injure for weeks, months, or years and then might suddenly start the behavior again. It is important that you do not take your friend's actions personally. Although occasionally a self-harmer's behavior may feel manipulative, it usually is not. Self-injury is a complex problem with many causes. It takes time and support for someone who has been self-injuring to heal emotionally.

It is very important to let an adult know if someone is self-harming. Do not help your friend keep the behavior a secret. Encourage your friend to talk to an adult, but if he or she refuses, then you must. This may be difficult to do, because it may seem to be a violation of trust. Your friend may become angry, and it may threaten your friendship. But suffering those consequences is

better than allowing your friend to continue to self-injure. Without someone intervening, your friend could cause serious—and potentially deadly—damage to his or her body.

Having a friend or family member who self-harms can be difficult. It is painful to realize that someone you care about deliberately hurts himself or herself. It is easy to understand why some people choose to ignore the warning signs and deny there is a problem. But standing by a friend, being available to talk, and providing alternatives to self-injury may provide the support your friend needs to stop the behavior and begin the healing process.

GLOSSARY

AESTHETIC Relating to beauty and how something appears.

AGGRAVATE To make worse.

BORDERLINE PERSONALITY DISORDER (BPD) A mental illness marked by unstable moods, behavior, relationships, and self-image.

COMPENSATE To make amends for; to counterbalance.

COMPULSION An irresistible impulse to perform an act.

CONFIDANT A person to whom secrets are entrusted.

COPE To deal with something that is difficult.

CYCLICAL Recurring in cycles; happening again and again.

ELECTIVE Beneficial to the patient but not essential for survival; optional.

IMPULSIVENESS The trait of acting suddenly without control, planning, or consideration of the consequences.

INTRUSIVE Unwelcome and disruptive.

IRRATIONAL Not reasonable or logical.

MISCONCEPTION An incorrect view or opinion.

NEUROTRANSMITTER A chemical that transmits nerve impulses from a nerve cell to another nerve cell, muscle, or gland.

POSTPARTUM DEPRESSION Clinical depression that affects some women shortly after pregnancy.

POST-TRAUMATIC STRESS DISORDER (PTSD) A psychological disorder that occurs after exposure to a highly stressful event or situation that is usually characterized by anxiety, depression, nightmares, and flashbacks.

PREVALENCE The percentage of a population that is affected by a disease at a given time.

SELF-INJURY The act of deliberately injuring or disfiguring one's own body.

SELF-PRESERVATION The natural tendency to act to protect oneself from harm or destruction.

SHOCK A life-threatening condition that occurs when the tissues and organs in the body are not receiving enough blood.

TRIGGER Something that causes symptoms to occur in a person who has a disease or illness.

TRAUMA An emotional wound or shock that has long-lasting effects on a person's psychological development.

TRICHOTILLOMANIA A psychological disorder in which a person compulsively pulls out his or her hair.

ULTIMATUM A final demand that, if rejected, will result in the end of a relationship or another serious consequence.

FOR MORE INFORMATION

American Self-Harm Information Clearinghouse (ASHIC)
521 Temple Place
Seattle, WA 98122
(206) 604-8963
Web site: http://www.selfinjury.org
The American Self-Harm Information Clearinghouse
provides information and awareness to medical and
psychological professionals and the general public
about self-injury.

Canadian Mental Health Association, Ontario
180 Dundas Street West, Suite 2301
Toronto, ON M5G 1Z8
Canada
(416) 977-5580
Web site: http://www.ontario.cmha.ca
The Canadian Mental Health Association, Ontario provides support and resources for those dealing with
mental health issues, such as depression and
thoughts of harming oneself.

Childhelp
15757 North 78th Street, Suite B
Scottsdale, AZ 85260
(480) 922-8212
Web site: http://www.childhelp.org
Childhelp is a national organization dedicated to ending
child abuse in America and around the world.

Cornell Research Program on Self-Injurious Behavior
(CRPSIB)
Bronfenbrenner Center for Translational Research
Beebe Hall
Cornell University
Ithaca, NY 14853
(607) 255-1861
Web site: http://www.crpsib.com
CRPSIB is a world leader in researching self-injuring
behaviors. Its Web site provides a wealth of information
as well as opportunities to participate in research.

Kids Help Phone
300-439 University Avenue
Toronto, ON M5G 1Y8
Canada
(800) 668-6868
Web site: http://www.kidshelpphone.ca
Kids Help Phone is a free and confidential service through
which children and youth can talk to counselors on the
phone or via the Web.

S.A.F.E. Alternatives
MacNeal Hospital
3249 South Oak Park Avenue
Berwyn, IL 60402
(800) DONTCUT [366-8288]
Web site: http://www.selfinjury.com

S.A.F.E. (Self Abuse Finally Ends) Alternatives works to educate people who self-injure about the dangers of their behaviors and empower them to make the correct decisions about stopping these behaviors.

WEB SITES

Due to the changing nature of Internet links, Rosen Publishing has developed an online list of Web sites related to the subject of this book. This site is updated regularly. Please use this link to access the list:

http://www.rosenlinks.com/HELP/Cut

FOR FURTHER READING

Allman, Toney. *Self-Injury* (Hot Topics). Detroit, MI: Lucent Books, 2011.

Eagen, Rachel. *Cutting and Self-Injury* (Straight Talk About—). New York, NY: Crabtree Publishing Company, 2011.

Friedman, Lauri S. *Self-Mutilation.* Detroit, MI: Greenhaven Press, 2009.

Hoban, Julia. *Willow*. New York, NY: Dial Books, 2009.

Hollander, Michael. *Helping Teens Who Cut: Understanding and Ending Self-Injury.* New York, NY: Guilford Press, 2008.

Oates, Joyce Carol. *Two or Three Things I Forgot to Tell You.* New York, NY: HarperTeen, 2012.

O'Neill, Terry. *Secret Scars: What You Need to Know About Cutting* (What's the Issue?). Mankato, MN: Compass Point Books, 2010.

Parks, Peggy J. *Self-Injury Disorder* (Compact Research: Diseases and Disorders). San Diego, CA: ReferencePoint Press, 2011.

Senker, Cath. *Self-Harm* (Teen Issues). Chicago, IL: Heinemann Library, 2013.

Shapiro, Lawrence E. *Stopping the Pain: A Workbook for Teens Who Cut & Self-Injure.* Oakland, CA: Instant Help Books, 2008.

Veague, Heather Barnett, and Christine E. Collins. *Cutting and Self-Harm* (Psychological Disorders). New York, NY: Chelsea House, 2008.

White, Tracy. *How I Made It to Eighteen: A Mostly True Story.* New York, NY: Roaring Brook Press, 2010.

Williams, Mary E. *Self-Mutilation* (Opposing Viewpoints). Detroit, MI: Greenhaven Press, 2008.

BIBLIOGRAPHY

BBC News. "The Panorama Interview." November 1995. Retrieved August 1, 2012 (http://www.bbc.co.uk/news/special/politics97/diana/panorama.html).

BBC News. "U.S. TV Airs Princess Diana Tapes." March 5, 2004. Retrieved August 1, 2012 (http://news.bbc.co.uk/2/hi/americas/3531997.stm).

Boudewyn, A. C., and J. H. Liem. "Childhood Sexual Abuse as a Precursor to Depression and Self-Destructive Behavior in Adulthood." *Journal of Traumatic Stress* 8 (1995): 445–449.

Brunel University. "True Extent of Self-Harm Amongst Teenagers Revealed." *ScienceDaily*, September 4, 2008. Retrieved July 29, 2012 (http://www.sciencedaily.com/releases/2008/09/080903101414.htm).

Centers for Disease Control and Prevention (CDC). "Traumatic Brain Injury." February 28, 2012. Retrieved August 9, 2012 (http://www.cdc.gov/TraumaticBrainInjury/index.html).

Cooper, Jayne, Navneet Kapur, Roger Webb, Martin Lawlor, Else Guthrie, Kevin Mackway-Jones, and Louis Appleby. "Suicide After Deliberate Self-Harm: A 4-Year Cohort Study." *American Journal of Psychiatry* 162 (2005): 297–303.

Dubo, Elyse D., Mary C. Zanarini, Ruth E. Lewis, and Amy A. Williams. "Childhood Antecedents of Self-Destructiveness in Borderline Personality Disorder." *Canadian Journal of Psychiatry* 42, no. 1 (1997): 63–69.

Favazza, Armando R. *Bodies Under Siege: Self-mutilation, Nonsuicidal Self-Injury, and Body*

Modification in Culture and Psychiatry. 3rd ed.
Baltimore, MD: Johns Hopkins University Press, 2011.

Marriott, Richard, Judith Horrocks, Allan House, and
David Owens. "Assessment and Management of
Self-Harm in Older Adults Attending Accident and
Emergency: A Comparative Cross-Sectional Study."
International Journal of Geriatric Psychiatry 18, no. 7
(July 2003): 645–652.

Motz, Anna, ed. *Managing Self-Harm: Psychological
Perspectives.* New York, NY: Routledge, 2009.

Mueser, Kim T., and Jonas Taub. "Trauma and PTSD
Among Adolescents with Severe Emotional Disorders
Involved in Multiple Service Systems." Psychiatric
Services, June 1, 2008. Retrieved August 9, 2012
(http://ps.psychiatryonline.org/article.aspx?Volume=59&
page=627&journalID=18).

Plante, Lori G. *Bleeding to Ease the Pain: Cutting, Self-
Injury, and the Adolescent Search for Self* (Abnormal
Psychology). Westport, CT: Praeger, 2007.

Whitlock, Janis, John Eckenrode, and Daniel Silverman.
"Self-Injurious Behaviors in a College Population."
Pediatrics 117, no. 6 (2006): 1939–1948.

Zoroya, Gregg. "Study Suggests Feelings of Guilt May Be
a Top Factor in PTSD." *USA Today*, November 25, 2011.
Retrieved August 9, 2012 (http://www.usatoday
.com/news/military/story/2011-11-23/
study-of-marines-ptsd/51386488/1).

ABOUT THE AUTHOR

John M. Shea has earned both a medical degree and a Ph.D. in biochemistry and molecular biology from the Medical University of South Carolina. He has always had a fascination with medicine and the science of how the body works. Recently, he has turned his attention to writing for children and young adults in the hope of sharing his enthusiasm for the wonders of human biology. When he is not writing health and science books, he can usually be found loudly cheering for the Buffalo Sabres.

PHOTO CREDITS

Cover © iStockphoto.com/Steve Debenport; pp. 5, 51 iStockphoto/ Thinkstock; pp. 8–9 Robert Ginn/Photolibrary/Getty Images; p. 11 D. Sharon Pruitt Pink Sherbet Photography/Flickr/Getty Images; p. 14 Carlos E. Santa Maria/Shutterstock.com; p. 17 Princess Diana Archive/ Hulton Royals Collection/ Getty Images; p. 18 Suzanne Tucker/ Shutterstock.com; p. 20 Christy Thompson/Shutterstock.com; p. 24 Hannamariah/Shutterstock.com; p. 26 Andreev Alexey/Shutterstock .com; p. 30 Tracy Whiteside/Shutterstock.com; p. 34 SW Productions/ Photodisc/Getty Images; p. 37 Jochen Schoenfeld/Shutterstock.com; p. 40 Charles Ommanney/Getty Images; p.43 Scott Camazine/Photo Researchers/Getty Images; pp. 46-47, 65 Peter Dazeley/Photographer's Choice/Getty Images; p. 53 Richard Clark/Photolibrary/Getty Images; p. 55 SW Productions/Stockbyte/Getty Images; p. 58 Ingram Publishing/ Thinkstock; pp. 62 LeoGrand/E+/Getty Images; p. 66 Klaus-Peter Wolf/ Getty Images; pp. 1, 7, 8–9, 13, 16–17, 23, 28, 32, 38, 42, 46–47, 49, 57, 60, 61, 64–65 background pattern (telephones) © iStockphoto.com/ Oksana Pasishnychenko; cover and interior telephone icons © iStockphoto.com/miniature.

Designer: Nicole Russo; Editor: Andrea Sclarow Paskoff;
Photo Researcher: Marty Levick